Author of

Don't Worry, He Won't Get Far on Foot:
The Autobiography of a Dangerous Man

Do Not Disturb Any Further

Digesting the Child Within:
And Other Cartoons to Live By

"Do what he says! He's crazy!!!"

Quill
William Morrow
New York

For information about Callahan T-shirts, mugs, and other products, please contact:

Levin Represents
Deborah Levin
P.O. Box 5575
Santa Monica, CA 90409

Copyright © 1992 by John Callahan

It is the policy of William Morrow and Company, Inc., and its imprints and affiliates, recognizing the importance of preserving what has been written, to print the books we publish on acid-free paper, and we exert our best efforts to that end.

Library of Congress Cataloging-in-Publication Data

Callahan, John.
     Do what he says! He's crazy!!! / by John Callahan.
       p. cm.
     ISBN 0-688-11815-1
     1. American wit and humor, Pictorial. I. Title.
NC1429.C23A4 1992
741.5′973—dc20   92-16272
                                             CIP

Printed in the United States of America

5 6 7 8 9 10

For Knucklehead Smith

I'd like to thank the following people for their unending help and support: Deborah Levin, Larry Wobbrock, Wendy Bellermann, Jerry Fine, Richard Pine, Francine Rose, and especially my editor, Liza Dawson, who *still* hasn't pushed me down the stairs.

It's a joke, it's a wildass joke.

—cellmate of John Callahan,
1969

"It's got to be silicone!"

CALLAHAN

"I should have known you'd be the needy one in this relationship!"

MADONNA'S CAT

CALLAHAN

CALLAHAN

CALLAHAN

CALLAHAN

"I'd like to talk about my abandonment issues."

CALLAHAN

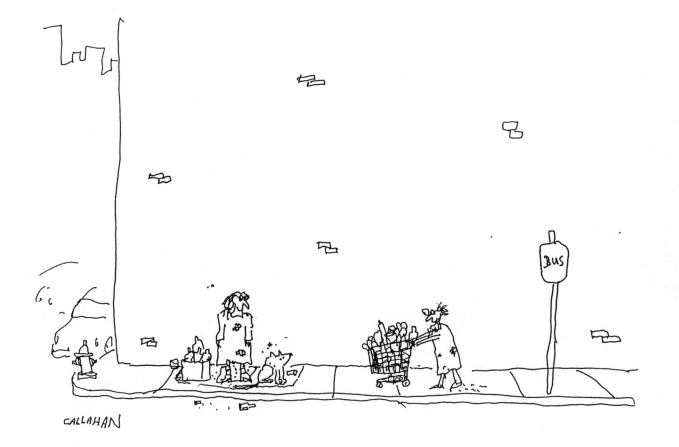

"Honey, I'm home!!"

"Now, class, is this man lying or laying in the gutter?"

"I'm thinking of making a bed and breakfast out
of it."

**"But, Monsieur! Our chef would never substitute
Shinola for the real thing!!!"**

CALLAHAN

"Perrier I presume?"

"In America, even a poor boy can grow up to win the
support of powerful special interest groups."

Let's talk about this compulsion to Reach for a can of spinach every time something goes wrong.
CALLAHAN

MADONNA'S COW

CALLAHAN

"This town ain't accessible enough for both of us!"

"See you Monday, Mr. Ronson, and by the way, I've *definitely concluded* that you *don't* have a multiple-personality problem!"

"How many times have I told you not to
stretch out that phone cord!!"

CALLAHAN

"The court sentences you to fifteen years in the
federal penitentiary with no possibility of TV movie."

"I'm sorry! I thought you said Cohens, not cones!"

CALLAHAN

DAN QUAYLE

CALLAHAN

THE MAN IN THE GREY FLANNEL CONDOM.

CALLAHAN

"You sure you don't want to come back tomorrow
when I'll have some more string?"

"Tie me up."

CALLAHAN

CALLAHAN

"This is a twenty-four-year-old male, who was
admitted last night with fever, chilling, and severe
abdominal cramping. . . ."

"Where did it all begin?"

CALLAHAN

"Well, it looks like the guests are beginning to trickle in."

"I warned you not to bring the beavers!"

"My client objects to the endless delays in this trial.
Attorney fees alone, he says, are becoming
increasingly painful to bear."

"Poor devil! That whale was *really* hard on him!"

CALLAHAN

**"He just hasn't been the same since he botched that
Elvis job!"**

CALLAHAN

HAPPY NEW YEAR!
THE HEMLOCK SOCIETY

CALLAHAN

"I won't be needing a bag."

CALLAHAN

"I'm gonna have to go with prize number three, Bob!"

"Oh, let him blow! It's not as bad as that Jehovah's
Witness wolf last week!"

CALLAHAN

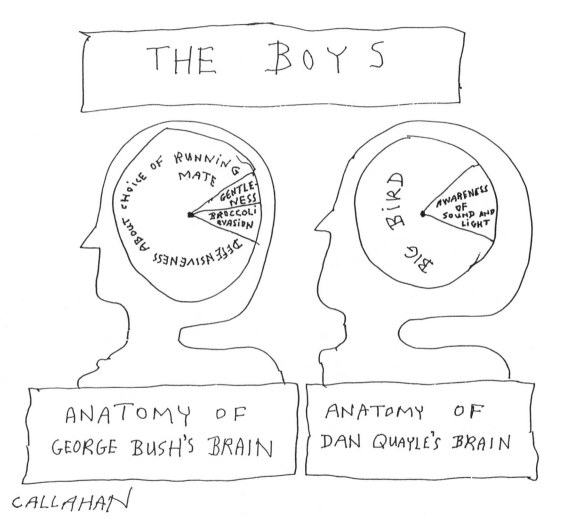

THE BOYS

ANATOMY OF
GEORGE BUSH'S BRAIN

ANATOMY OF
DAN QUAYLE'S BRAIN

CALLAHAN

CALLAHAN

CALLAHAN

MOONA LISA

CALLAHAN

CALLAHAN

CALLAHAN

"Miss Jones, please unplug the intercom!!!"

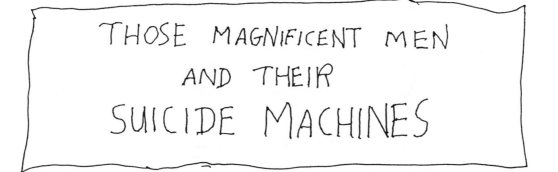

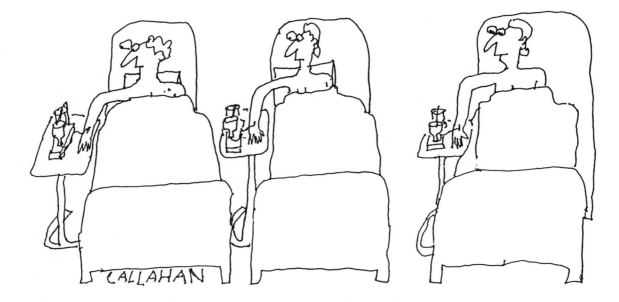

CALLAHAN

"Doesn't he look natural?"

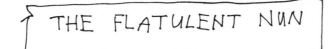

THE FLATULENT NUN

CALLAHAN

"What's all this talk about pollutants in
Santa Monica bay!"

PICASSO SNAPS A BACKYARD PHOTO

CALLAHAN

"Okay, everybody. . . . one eye over the other and an extra mouth!"

This is a piece I wrote a couple of years ago, almost as an attempt to work out some personal conflicts. When I showed it to my dad he just said, "Real good, Johnny, your mom wants to talk to you."

Dad

By John Callahan

**My dad was a disciplinarian from the
outset.**

**After Kip and I were born, he was
tender and loving.**

**Dad took over when Mom was in the
hospital having more babies.**

My dad was a war hero but he didn't talk much about it.

**One time, returning from the beach,
my cousin and all the Callahans got
sick.**

**Every Sunday before confession Dad
gave us flattop haircuts.**

After finishing, he sent us upstairs for our mother's approval.

Saturday evenings Dad walked us to confession.

**At Mass the next morning, he always
fell asleep during the sermon.**

**After Mass, Dad drove us to
Grandpa's to visit Grandma who'd
had a stroke.**

Sometimes Dad stopped at the Dairy
Queen on the way back home.

Dad was a hardworking man and
often nodded off on Sunday
afternoon.

Sometimes Sparkie's barking
awakened Dad.

**On Christmas Eve 1960, Grandpa
Joe died in a freeway accident while
delivering bicycles for us kids.**

I was the only one of the children
Dad took to the funeral.

**Dad always provided us with a
weekly allowance.**

He took care to impart proper social etiquette.

**Dad took Kip and me aside to
explain the facts of life.**

**Growing into adolescence, I became
rebellious and resentful toward Dad.**

Once at a birthday party I went too
far and Dad exploded.

Our relationship deteriorated.

Even today, though we are friendly,
a certain lack of communication still
exists.

**I often wonder if I will raise my
children the same way Dad raised me.**

I think I'd prefer to die before my father to avoid the grief of his passing.